This Journal Belongs To...................................

12 weeks

A 12 weeks Guide Toward Self-Empowerment For Women

Printed in the United States of America
ISBN: 978-1-7321362-2-9

Written by Reea Rodney
Cover Design by Alaxandra Gold
Designed by FindlayCreative.com

This 12 week Guide is
dedicated to all Women EVERYWHERE!

Please use this link to download a Free
Goal Setting Worksheet Kit:
www.coachreea.com/goal-setting-
activity

12 weeks

A 12 weeks Guide Toward Self-Empowerment For Women

Written by
Coach Reea Rodney

A 12 Weeks Guide Toward Self-Empowerment For Women

Table of Contents

12 weeks

A 12 Weeks Guide Toward Self-Empowerment For Women

INTRODUCTION

Julius Erving once quipped, "The key to success is to keep growing in all areas of life - mental, emotional, spiritual, as well as physical." This philosophy is what has guided Life Coach, Reea Rodney, to author several books which helps individuals become their better selves. Now, Rodney has come up with an innovative way to further empower her readers. In the Learning How to Empower Myself journal, readers are encouraged to journal with purpose.

Researchers have provided many benefits to journaling. Some include: self-awareness, stress reliever, encourage positive thinking, better decision making, and more.

This 12 week journal is filled with lessons on affirmations and how these can help identify areas for improvement, build self-esteem, and cultivate positive thinking and attitude. For maximum impact, readers are encouraged to apply as much of the tools from the journal and commit themselves to journaling at least once a day for the next 12 weeks.

It's time to delve into the various lessons. Remember, it's fine to take care of yourself!

PURPOSE

USING THIS JOURNALING GUIDE

"A Personal Journal is an ideal environment in which to "Become." It is a perfect place for you to THINK, FEEL, DISCOVER, EXPAND, REMEMBER, and DREAM."

~ Brad Wilcox

This is a 12 weeks guide towards self-empowerment for women. Take a moment each day to journal in this book by answering the questions presented. Quotes from wonderful people through out history and encouraging words of affirmation will be presented for you to ponder, think, rememinise about, all in the hopes that this guide will help you learn more about who you are as a person - a very worthy and precious person.

And remember. You are here right now -

Learning How To Empower Yourself

You are
BRAVE

You are
LOVED

You are
NOT
ALONE

I EMPOWER ME PLEDGE

I Pledge to **EMPOWER ME** to
the best of my Ability.
Every morning when I Rise,
I **EMPOWER** my Mind
I **EMPOWER** my Body
I **EMPOWER** my Soul
I **EMPOWER** my Vision
I **EMPOWER** my Actions
And I **EMPOWER** my
Conversations
I **EMPOWER** the words that are
spoken aloud, and the
silent ones in my head.
I am loving and kind to the
person I see in the mirror
looking back at me.
Because
I **EMPOWER ME!**

~ Reea Rodney

Every morning read aloud this pledge. Make the
commitment to empower yourself and become the
best you, you were created to be.

WEEK ONE FOCUS: SELF-DISCOVERY

There's so much that can be said about self-discovery. One of the significant factors of discovering yourself is the realization that you must be discovered. Often people tend to brush off the idea of self-discovery for several reasons: they may feel it is pointless, they're unable to see how the results of self-discovery would help them in their journey, or they don't believe that they have not discovered who they are. Whatever the reason, here are just a few reasons to take the time to discover yourself:

- We naturally evolve, so your thought process and understanding of life also evolves.
- Knowing your authentic self reduces the potential for low self-esteem.
- It is a confidence booster.
- It gives us the gage in which we should experience life.
- It ensures you eliminate the mask you may be wearing and show the world your beautiful and authentic self.

For the next couple of days, take the time to explore several areas of your life. Think of how these things have made an impact on who you have become. In the end, write the things you have discovered about yourself.

WHEN I
DISCOVER
WHO I AM
I'LL BE
FREE

~Ralph Ellison

DAY ONE: SELF - DISCOVERY

1. Think about what the phrase "Self - Discovery" means to you.
   Write down your thoughts...

   _____

   _____

   _____

   _____

2. What things did you enjoy discovering as a child? How have
   these discoveries changed over the years?

   _____

   _____

   _____

DAY TWO: SELF - DISCOVERY

1. If you could have dinner with anyone currently alive, who would it be and why?

_____

_____

_____

_____

2. If you could meet any fictional character - book, myth or movie - who would it be and why?

_____

_____

_____

_____

"You're off to Great Places!
Today is your day!
Your mountain is waiting,
So... get on your way!"

~ Dr. Seuss, Oh, The Places You'll Go!

DAY THREE: SELF - DISCOVERY

1. Make a list of 30 things that makes you smile.

1 _____

2 _____

3 _____

4 _____

5 _____

6 _____

7 _____

8 _____

9 _____

10 _____

11 _____

12 _____

13 _____

14 _____

15 _____

16 _____

17 _____

18 _____

19 _____

20 _____

21 _____

22 _____

23 _____

24 _____

25 _____

26 _____

27 _____

28 _____

29 _____

30 _____

DAY FOUR: SELF - DISCOVERY

"Being able to **identify** yourself by **knowing** who you are, what you **believe** in, and **where** you want to go is one of the most **courageous** things you can do."

1. What do you think the author means by their inspirational quote above?

_____

_____

_____

2. How do you think that applies to your life, your circumstances, your dreams, your family and friends?

_____

_____

_____

_____

DAY FIVE: SELF - DISCOVERY

THE MOST...   (Fill in the blanks)

The most terrifying moment of my life was _____

_____

_____

The most fun I've ever had _____

_____

_____

The most surprised I've ever been _____

_____

_____

The most disappointed I've ever been _____

_____

_____

The most actiity I was looking forward to _____

_____

_____

DAY SIX: SELF - DISCOVERY

For I know the

PLANS

I have for you, declares the LORD. Plans to

PROSPER

you and not to harm you, plans to give you hope and a

FUTURE

~ Jeremiah 29:11

What would you like your future to look like?

_____

_____

_____

END OF THE WEEK JOURNAL

1. what did you discover about yourself this week?

_____

_____

_____

2. what areas will you improve?

_____

_____

_____

3. what goals have you set as a result of this week's lesson?

_____

_____

_____

4. What steps will you take to achieve your goals?

_____

_____

_____

5. Are you committed to achieving your goals, If yes why?

_____

_____

_____

_____

WEEK TWO FOCUS: SELF-TALK

Proverbs 18:21 states "Death and life are in the power of the tongue..." (KJV). Words are powerful, and you must be sure to use them wisely. What you say to yourself (and others) can bring positive or negative results. This week, you will delve in more on this topic and develop a script that you can use to shape your life. Be sure to think positive and don't shy from speaking to yourself aloud.

Remember, words are powerful, so the more you speak positivity to yourself, the better you will become. By the end of this week, you will identify some areas of negativity and replace them with positive ones. The goal must always be to have a positive outlook of yourself.

I am
UNIQUELY
made and exceptionally
BEAUTIFUL

~ Reea Rodney

DAY ONE: SELF - TALK

1. If I could talk to my teenage self, the one thing I would say is...

_____

_____

_____

_____

2. The words I'd like to live by are...

_____

_____

_____

DAY TWO: SELF - TALK

Dear Me...

Write a letter of encouragement to yourself as if from your future self. If this is hard to do, think about writing to your daughter or your loved one, only the letter is for you.

DAY THREE: SELF - TALK

1. Make a list of 30 things that describes you best.

1 _____   16 _____

2 _____   17 _____

3 _____   18 _____

4 _____   19 _____

5 _____   20 _____

6 _____   21 _____

7 _____   22 _____

8 _____   23 _____

9 _____   24 _____

10 _____   25 _____

11 _____   26 _____

12 _____   27 _____

13 _____   28 _____

14 _____   29 _____

15 _____   30 _____

DAY FOUR: SELF - TALK

"Your **Self-Talk** conversations are the most **powerful** conversations you'll ever have. They can **empower** you to do **great** things or they can **sabotage** your every **step**."

~ Reea Rodney

1. What negative or defeating words am I often saying about myself or to myself?

_____

_____

_____

_____

2. Which of these words can be replaced with something more positive? Write down replacement words for you to use about yourself.

_____

_____

_____

_____

DAY FIVE: SELF - TALK

THE MOST...   (Fill in the blanks)

The most negative words I tell myself are...

_____

_____

The most postitive words I speak over myself are...

_____

_____

The most empowering words I use for me are...

_____

_____

The most fun self-talk I use is...

_____

_____

The most truthful words I tell myself are...

_____

_____

DAY SIX: SELF - TALK

"What you confess
with your

mouth

is what you will bring
into your reality.
If you think you can
or can't, that is
what it will be."

what have you been telling yourself you can't do? Is it true?

_____

_____

_____

_____

END OF THE WEEK JOURNAL

1. What did you learn about yourself this week?

_____

_____

_____

2. What areas will you improve?

_____

_____

_____

3. What goals have you set as a result of this week's lesson?

_____

_____

_____

4. What steps will you take to achieve your goals?

_____

_____

_____

5. Are you committed to achieving your goals, If yes why?

_____

_____

_____

_____

_____

WEEK TWO: SELF - TALK

WEEK THREE FOCUS: SELF-LOVE

There's something powerful about self-love. When we love ourselves, our outlook on life, our attitude towards ourselves and others is positive. More importantly, self-love helps us to discover more about ourselves.

Could you imagine what the world would be like if everyone loved themselves? Their positive outlook alone would better our society and the way we treat each other.

This week explore your experiences on love and consider how this has impacted you. Then think on how you can develop or improve on how you love yourself.

To be in love with
YOURSELF
is one of the
greatest love
affairs you
can ever
experience

~Reea Rodney

DAY ONE: SELF - LOVE

What does unconditional love look like for you?

_____

_____

_____

_____

What would you do if you loved yourself unconditionally? How
can you act on these things, whether you do or don't?

_____

_____

_____

_____

DAY TWO: SELF - LOVE

1. What do you love about life?

_____

_____

_____

_____

_____

2. What always brings tears to your eyes? What is important to you?

_____

_____

_____

_____

_____

> "Be **faithful** to **yourself** and **love** you like no one else **ever** could."
>
> ~ Reea Rodney

DAY THREE: SELF - LOVE

1. Make a list of 30 things that you love about yourself.

1	16
2	17
3	18
4	19
5	20
6	21
7	22
8	23
9	24
10	25
11	26
12	27
13	28
14	29
15	30

DAY FOUR: SELF - LOVE

"Self-Love is **indeed** the **greatest** love of all. Spend time **loving** yourself and watch how **everything** else **falls** into place at the **right** time."

1. What are your thoughts about this inspirational statement? Do you agree?

_____

_____

_____

_____

2. What do you think loving yourself first looks like to you?

_____

_____

_____

_____

_____

DAY FIVE: SELF - LOVE

THE TIME I...   (Fill in the blanks)

The time I felt most loved was...

The time I most enjoyed being myself was...

The time I felt most happy was...

The time I most loved myself was...

The time I felt most content was...

DAY SIX: SELF - LOVE

SHE
is clothed in
STRENGTH
and dignity, and she
LAUGHS
without fear of the future.
~ Proverbs 31:25

Which of your personal strengths do you love the most?

_____

_____

_____

_____

END OF THE WEEK JOURNAL

1. What did you discover about yourself this week?

_____

_____

2. What areas will you improve?

_____

_____

3. What goals have you set as a result of this week's lesson?

_____

_____

4. What steps will you take to achieve your goals?

_____

_____

5. Are you committed to achieving your goals, If yes why?

_____

_____

_____

_____

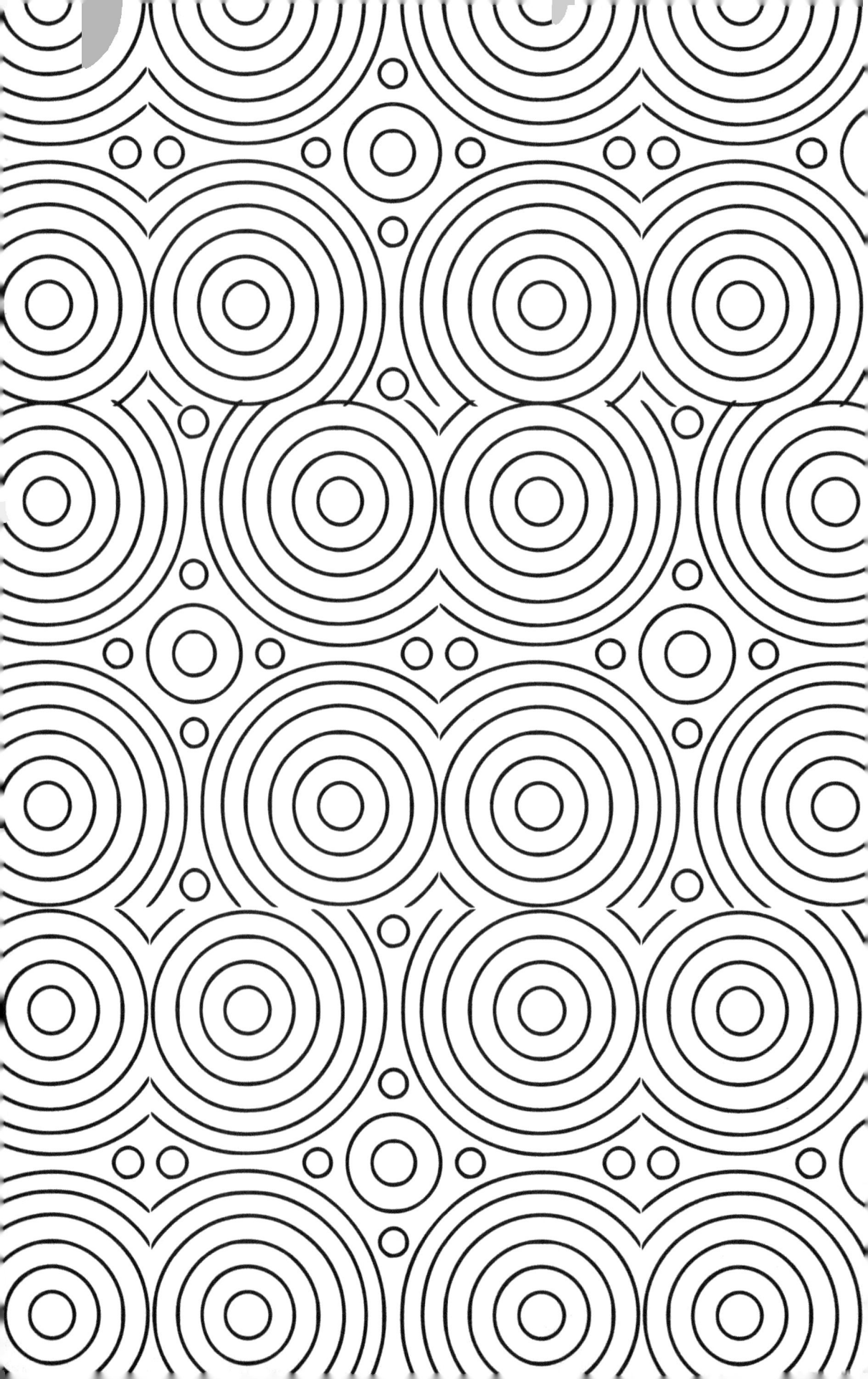

WEEK FOUR FOCUS: SELF-CARE

Self-care covers a broad spectrum of things. For the sake of this journal, we will consider the following areas:

- Physical
- Mental
- Spiritual

How would you rate how well you take care of yourself? The goal of this chapter is to identify room for improvement. For instance, are you allowing yourself to have some "me" time? Are you investing in your future? Do you exercise regularly? Do you pray and meditate on a regular basis?

In other words, are you genuinely caring for yourself?

"Beauty starts from within; take care of your spiritual **BEAUTY** and watch your light shine **BRIGHTLY** for all to see."

DAY ONE: SELF - CARE

1. What does self-care look like for you?

_____

_____

_____

_____

2. When you care for yourself and manage your self-care well, how does it make you feel?

_____

_____

_____

_____

DAY TWO: SELF - CARE

1. Make a list of 30 things that you can do for your personal self-care.

1	16
2	17
3	18
4	19
5	20
6	21
7	22
8	23
9	24
10	25
11	26
12	27
13	28
14	29
15	30

DAY THREE: SELF - CARE

What were some of the things you used to do that helped you take care of you? What stopped you from continuing to do these activites?

_____

_____

_____

_____

_____

How could you arrange your daily and weekly schedule to include self-care activities and action? In what areas of your life do you need to make changes?

_____

_____

_____

_____

DAY FOUR: SELF - CARE

"Self-care is the **best** care. Take time to **replenish** your **body, mind, and spirit** - and remember to **serve** from your **overflow**."

~ Reea Rodney

Describe a time when you tried serving while running on "empty". What do you think you could have done differently with your self-care? How do you think this could have helped?

DAY FIVE: SELF - CARE

When I am...
(Fill in the blanks with self-care actions)

When I am tired, I can...

_____

_____

When I am overwhelmed, I need to...

_____

_____

When I am content I could...

_____

_____

When I am fearful I should...

_____

_____

When I am busy I can...

_____

_____

When I have time I should try...

_____

_____

DAY SIX: SELF - CARE

"Caring for yourself should be your number one priority. It's no one else's job to take care of you

BUT YOU

Why do you think the responsibility for self-care is yours?

_____

_____

_____

What time in your day or week do you have for self-care?

_____

_____

_____

END OF THE WEEK JOURNAL

1. What did you discover about yourself this week?

_____

_____

_____

2. What areas will you improve?

_____

_____

_____

3. What goals have you set as a result of this week's lesson?

_____

_____

_____

4. What steps will you take to achieve your goals?

_____

_____

_____

5. Are you committed to achieving your goals, If yes why?

_____

_____

_____

_____

WEEK FOUR: SELF - CARE

ABOUT AFFIRMATIONS

The key, when saying or reading affirmations, is to allow yourself to feel an emotional connection to the words or statements you are saying. Try to relax and allow yourself to be at a place of peace and tranquility. You must identify these statements as being truthful and accurate. If you're having trouble connecting because they feel out of reach or you simply can't see yourself in that space, you can adjust the affirmation to include the words that would make you connect more until you can see yourself in that way.

Also, affirmations can become a powerful tool for personal development and mindset, but repetition must be an essential part of the process. The more often you say them, the more they will impact your reality. Affirmations are not intended to be used occasionally, it's an everyday choice. It's a decision we make with our thoughts and feelings. The more often you use affirmations, the faster you will begin to see new opportunities, engage in new healthy behaviors, live your life with purpose each day and feel energized by the direction your life will be taking.

Affirmation Definition:
1. The assertion that something exists or is true.
2. Something that is affirmed; a statement or proposition that is declared to be true.
3. Confirmation or ratification of the truth or validity of a prior judgment, decision, etc.
4. A solemn declaration accepted instead of a statement under oath.

Additionally, "I AM" is said to be the single most powerful statement in the English Language. When you say I AM and combine it with a positive word, your subconscious WILL instantly begin to agree with you once you truly believe you can achieve your statement.

Powerful "I Am" Statements

1. I am uniquely made and exceptionally beautiful.

2. I am worthy of love.

3. I am strong.

4. I am more than enough.

5. I am victorious.

6. I am an awesome friend.

7. I am fearless, selfless and destined for greatness.

8. I am more than a conqueror.

9. I am faithful to my purpose.

10. I am the definition of love.

WEEK EIGHT: CREATIVITY

WEEK FIVE FOCUS: SELF-EMPOWERMENT

This week consider all that you've explored and learned about yourself so far. Think of the changes you've made to move in a more positive direction in your life. Seriously, think of it (whether big or small). Now...congratulate yourself!

You should be proud of your accomplishments. Be sure to use that sense of pride to empower yourself. Need a bit more motivation? No worries; this week's entries should help you through your journey to self-empowerment.

"You have the **POWER** and the **ABILITY** to empower yourself from deep within."

~ Reea Rodney

DAY ONE: SELF - EMPOWERMENT

1. What does Self-Empowerment mean to you?

_____

_____

_____

_____

2. What things do you already do for Self-Empowerment?

_____

_____

_____

_____

DAY TWO: SELF - EMPOWERMENT

1. If God had one key life question for you, for which the answer would give your life purpose, what would it be?

_____

_____

_____

_____

_____

2. If you wrote your own book, straight from your heart, what would the book's title be? What would you cover in the 7 main chapters? We are all here to give back in some way.

_____

_____

_____

_____

"**Worry not** about if you fail but be focus and **understand** that in the midst of failure there's the **Gift of Knowledge**."

~ Reea Rodney

DAY THREE: SELF - EMPOWERMENT

1. Make a list of 30 encouraging truths about yourself.

1	16
2	17
3	18
4	19
5	20
6	21
7	22
8	23
9	24
10	25
11	26
12	27
13	28
14	29
15	30

DAY FOUR: SELF - EMPOWERMENT

"The day I **freed** myself from my self-defeated **mindset** and destructive patterns was the most **liberating** day of my **life.**"

1. What are some of the destructive patterns you can free yourself from?

_____

_____

_____

2. What truths or actions can you replace your self-defeated mindset with?

_____

_____

_____

DAY FIVE: SELF - EMPOWERMENT

What makes you, YOU?

What makes you unique? _____

_____

_____

How do you stand out from the crowd? _____

_____

_____

What are your best character traits? _____

_____

_____

What are you really good at? _____

_____

_____

What challenges you the most? _____

_____

_____

DAY SIX: SELF - EMPOWERMENT

"EMPOWERMENT
means taking
RESPONSIBILITY
It's never about
blaming others."

~ Reea Rodey

Who are the people in my life that are supportive and will help me nurture my dreams and goals? How can I spend more time with them?

_____

_____

_____

_____

_____

_____

_____

END OF THE WEEK JOURNAL

1. What did you discover about yourself this week?

2. What areas will you improve?

3. What goals have you set as a result of this week's lesson?

4. What steps will you take to achieve your goals?

5. Are you committed to achieving your goals, If yes why?

WEEK SIX FOCUS: SELF-CONFIDENCE

Can you think of someone who is confident in themselves? What does that look like? Perhaps it's the way they carry themselves. Maybe it's the clothes they wear. Or could it be their intellect? Whatever it is, know this...EVERYONE HAS FLAWS!

However, how you address your flaws may impact how you feel about yourself.

As always, this week, you will reflect on your personal experiences, identify what self-confidence is to you, and think of how to achieve this.

Because I'm confident in

MYSELF

and my abilities, I'll be

FINE

even if they don't like me for me.

DAY ONE: SELF - CONFIDENCE

1. What does self-confidence look like in your life?

_____

_____

_____

_____

2. In what areas of your life would you like more self-confidence?

_____

_____

_____

_____

_____

DAY TWO: SELF - CONFIDENCE

1. Make a list of 30 ways you can boost your own self-confidence:

1 _____
2 _____
3 _____
4 _____
5 _____
6 _____
7 _____
8 _____
9 _____
10 _____
11 _____
12 _____
13 _____
14 _____
15 _____

16 _____
17 _____
18 _____
19 _____
20 _____
21 _____
22 _____
23 _____
24 _____
25 _____
26 _____
27 _____
28 _____
29 _____
30 _____

DAY THREE: SELF - CONFIDENCE

What changes can I make to develop a stronger relationship with myself? What perceived "flaws" do I need to overcome so that I can get closer to self-acceptance and confidence?

_____

_____

_____

_____

_____

What relationship problems exist (with family, friends, coworkers)? What are my options to overcome them?

_____

_____

_____

_____

DAY FOUR: SELF - CONFIDENCE

"The **essential** lessons I've **learned** in life is to just be yourself and to **treasure** the **remarkable** and **unique** being that **you** are."

What do you think about the inspirational quote above? Do you agree?

_____

_____

_____

_____

_____

_____

_____

_____

DAY FIVE: SELF - CONFIDENCE

The Most...

(Fill in the blanks)

The most confident I've ever felt was... _____
_____
_____

The most proud of myself was when... _____
_____
_____

The greatest achievement of mine was... _____
_____
_____

My biggest breakthrough moment was... _____
_____
_____

A moment of great positive impact on my life was... _____
_____
_____
_____
_____

DAY SIX: SELF - CONFIDENCE

Self-confidence is the best outfit:

ROCK IT
and
OWN IT!

what has the fear of failure stopped you from doing? Can you think of one step you could take today to begin overcoming that fear to gain confidence?

_____

_____

_____

_____

END OF THE WEEK JOURNAL

1. What did you learn about yourself this week?

_____

_____

_____

2. What areas will you improve?

_____

_____

_____

3. What goals have you set as a result of this week's lesson?

_____

_____

_____

4. What steps will you take to achieve your goals?

_____

_____

_____

5. Are you committed to achieving your goals, If yes why?

_____

_____

_____

_____

_____

WEEK SIX: SELF - CONFIDENCE

WEEK SEVEN FOCUS: COURAGE

Courage is the ability to face something you fear – at least that's how I define it. This week think of what courage means to you. Then think of the times you didn't feel courageous. Now, what caused you not to be courageous in those moments? What could you have done differently?

A lot to think about, right? Well, don't worry. Take the time to define courage, explore life experiences, and determine what steps you will take to be courageous.

COURAGE

is like a

muscle. We

STRENGTHEN

it by use."

~Ruth Gordo

DAY ONE: COURAGE

1. What does courage look like for you?

_____

_____

_____

2. Describe a time you were proud for being brave and courageous.

_____

_____

_____

DAY TWO: COURAGE

1. If you could change one thing about your present life, what would it be?

_____

_____

_____

2. If you could live anywhere you wanted, where would you live?

_____

_____

_____

3. If you could go back in time and change one thing from your past, what would it be?

_____

_____

_____

"Don't be afraid to **say** what you **want** because you'll be **holding yourself** back from **receiving** it "

~ Reea Rodney

DAY THREE: COURAGE

1. Make a list of 30 ways you can be courageous.

1 _____   16 _____

2 _____   17 _____

3 _____   18 _____

4 _____   19 _____

5 _____   20 _____

6 _____   21 _____

7 _____   22 _____

8 _____   23 _____

9 _____   24 _____

10 _____   25 _____

11 _____   26 _____

12 _____   27 _____

13 _____   28 _____

14 _____   29 _____

15 _____   30 _____

DAY FOUR: COURAGE

"I was once **afraid** of people saying "Who does she **think** she is? Now I have the courage to **stand** and **say**, "This is who I am!"
~ Oprah Winfrey

1. What do you think Oprah Winfrey meant by her quote above?

_____

_____

_____

_____

2. In what areas of your life will you stand and say "This is who I am"?

_____

_____

_____

_____

_____

DAY FIVE: COURAGE

Write a letter:

Write a letter to someone who **encouraged** and believed in you, even when you didn't believe in yourself.

DAY SIX: COURAGE

Be of good **courage**
and He shall strengthen your

HEART

all you who

HOPE

in the LORD.
~ Psalms 31:24

Was there a time in your life when you felt God had strengthened
your heart and fortified your courage?

_____

_____

_____

_____

END OF THE WEEK JOURNAL

1. What did you learn about yourself this week?

2. What areas will you improve?

3. What goals have you set as a result of this week's lesson?

4. What steps will you take to achieve your goals?

5. Are you committed to achieving your goals, If yes why?

WEEK EIGHT FOCUS: CREATIVITY

Creativity is a powerful way to embrace your uniqueness. Creativity is not limited to making things; it is more about growing. When we grow, it helps us discover the vibrant and lively world we live in. Our surrounding appears different. In fact, our level of motivation also increases.

Creativity helps us find ways to overcome obstacles and roadblocks in our lives. It helps develop new opportunities in overcoming these obstacles. We are natural problem solvers — some more than others. This week you will identify how you express yourself, what you love to do, your dreams, and how you have and will continue to grow.

Be sure to have fun this week...and **be creative!**

CREATE A LIFE

that feels good on the inside, not just look good on the outside.

DAY ONE: CREATIVITY

1. What creative activities do you use to express yourself?

_____

_____

_____

_____

2. What do you try to achieve with your creativity?

_____

_____

_____

_____

_____

DAY TWO: CREATIVITY

1. Make a list of 30 things that you can do that express your creativity.

1 _____

2 _____

3 _____

4 _____

5 _____

6 _____

7 _____

8 _____

9 _____

10 _____

11 _____

12 _____

13 _____

14 _____

15 _____

16 _____

17 _____

18 _____

19 _____

20 _____

21 _____

22 _____

23 _____

24 _____

25 _____

26 _____

27 _____

28 _____

29 _____

30 _____

DAY THREE: CREATIVITY

Creativity emerges the moment our imagination awakens and we feel joy doing something we love. What do you love to do?

_____

_____

_____

_____

_____

What have been the most creative times in your life? How were you able to grow during these times?

_____

_____

_____

DAY FOUR: CREATIVITY

"**Creativity** is how I **share** my **heart, soul** and **talent** with the **universe.**"

~ Reea Rodney

When you were a child, how did you share your soul through creativity?

_____

_____

How has your creativity helped sculpt your life, your expression of yourself, and your dreams?

_____

_____

_____

_____

_____

_____

DAY FIVE: CREATIVITY

My Dreams...
(Fill in the bubbles with your goals and dreams)

When I was a
child I dreamed of...

_____

_____

_____

_____

I long to see my
family achieve...

_____

_____

_____

_____

If I could I
would...

_____

_____

_____

When I get the
chance I want to...

_____

_____

_____

The thing that
gets me most
excited is...

_____

_____

_____

DAY SIX: CREATIVITY

For we are his
workmanship,
created in Christ Jesus
to **good works,**
which God has before
ordained that we
should walk in them.
~ Ephesians 2:10

What do you believe is your creative skill or ability? In what ways do you utilize them at work or at home?

END OF THE WEEK JOURNAL

1. What did you learn about yourself this week?

_____

_____

_____

2. What areas will you improve?

_____

_____

_____

3. What goals have you set as a result of this week's lesson?

_____

_____

_____

4. What steps will you take to achieve your goals?

_____

_____

_____

5. Are you committed to achieving your goals, If yes why?

_____

_____

_____

_____

WEEK EIGHT: CREATIVITY

Inspirational Affirmations for Personal Development

1. My body is healthy; my mind is brilliant; my soul is at peace.

2. I am superior to the negative thoughts and low actions.

3. Creative energy surges through me and leads me to new and brilliant ideas.

4. I chose to be happy. Consider your accomplishments and the blessings you've been given.

5. My thoughts are filled with positivity, and my life is overflowing with prosperity.

6. Today, I release myself from old habits and take up new and more positive ones.

7. Many people look up to me and recognize my worth; I am admired.

8. I acknowledge my self-worth; my confidence is soaring.

9. Everything that is happening now is happening for my ultimate good.

10. I am a powerhouse; I am indestructible.

Inspirational Affirmations for Personal Development

11. Never let the hand you hold, hold you down. ~ Unknown Author.

12. Its your time to Jump. Take that leap of Faith in You and Go for it.

13. You miss 100% of the shots you don't take. Believe in you and Jump...

14. Life is what happens to you when you're busy making other plans.

15. Don't look back. You're not going that way.

16. Your time is limited, so don't waste it living someone else's life. Be You, Do You.

17. Look at the stars. Look how they shine just for you.

18. Don't worry if you're not where you want to be yet. Great things take time.

19. Strive not to be a success, but rather to be of great value.

20. Overcoming obstacles made me the person I am today. What obstacle have you overcome?

INSPIRATIONAL AFFIRMATIONS

WEEK NINE FOCUS: BODY PROUD

By now, you should've learned more about yourself, identified areas for improvement, and embraced who you are. This week is a doozie as you will be asked to embrace an area where many people struggle with — your body. That's right! This week is all about Body Proud.

You. Are. Beautiful.

Everyone was created differently, yet often times, people tend to wish they looked like someone else...well, what's wrong with you? Nothing! You are beautiful. So, what, you have to shed a few pounds. You are beautiful. So, what, you're "too short/too tall?" You are beautiful. Ok, ...so you don't have the perfect set of teeth.

YOU ARE BEAUTIFUL!

No matter your supposed flaws, if you don't learn to embrace your body, there's no guarantee you'll truly embrace who you are once you've "fixed" your flaws. Let's be Body Proud this week and beyond.

"You are beautiful just the way **YOU ARE** and stronger than you think."

~Reea Rodney

WEEK NINE: BODY PROUD

DAY ONE: BODY PROUD

1. How would you explain to your friend or daughter about being proud of their body?

_____

_____

_____

2. If you could change one thing about your body, what would it be?

_____

_____

_____

3. If you couldn't change that one thing, how could you be proud of it anyway?

_____

_____

DAY TWO: BODY PROUD

1. Make a list of 30 things that you love about your body.

1	16
2	17
3	18
4	19
5	20
6	21
7	22
8	23
9	24
10	25
11	26
12	27
13	28
14	29
15	30

DAY THREE: BODY PROUD

What are three things you like about the way you look?

_____

_____

_____

_____

Name three things you like about yourself that have nothing to
do with what you look like.

_____

_____

_____

_____

Take **care** of yourself. **Eat well.**
Rest and train **hard** and **smart.**
Make **time** to think and breathe.
Be **intentional** with your time.
~ Kristin Armstrong

DAY FOUR: BODY PROUD

What makes you, YOU?
What makes you unique?

How do you stand out from the crowd?

How would you describe yourself?

How would your best friend describe you?

How would you descirbe your favorite thing about your body?

What stops you from caring for your body?

What can you do to change this?

DAY FIVE: BODY PROUD

Write a letter:

Write a letter to your younger self, warning her about the impacts of not being body proud.

DAY SIX: BODY PROUD

I will empower my

MIND
BODY
AND SOUL

What are some ways that you can empower your mind, body and your soul?

_____

_____

_____

_____

_____

_____

END OF THE WEEK JOURNAL

1. What did you learn about yourself this week?

2. What areas will you improve?

3. What goals have you set as a result of this week's lesson?

4. What steps will you take to achieve your goals?

5. Are you committed to achieving your goals, If yes why?

WEEK TEN FOCUS: CELEBRATING YOU

Let me let you in on a little secret – celebrating myself has been an area I've struggled with for some time. With the hustle and bustle of life, managing a household, working, and achieving my goals, taking time to celebrate "me" can be a challenge. But I've learned that taking time to celebrate and invest in myself is extremely important.

Celebrating You allows you to enjoy the journey of life. Ever had a goal you wanted to achieve? Why celebrate once you've accomplished your goal? Why not celebrate every step of the journey? In the end, you will appreciate your achievement (and yourself) even more. Celebrating You increases your self-confidence. With confidence, you are unstoppable. Your outlook on life becomes more focused, and your stress level will be reduced, significantly.

Celebrate You every day...you deserve it!

"Pause for a moment and realize how much **PROGRESS** you have made. Be **PROUD** of yourself; celebrate yourself."

~Roxana Jones

DAY ONE: CELEBRATING YOU

1. What do you think it means to celebrate yourself?

_____

_____

_____

_____

_____

2. How do you like to celebrate yourself? What are some of the things you do?

_____

_____

_____

_____

DAY TWO: CELEBRATING YOU

1. Make a list of 30 ways that you can celebrate you.

1 _____
2 _____
3 _____
4 _____
5 _____
6 _____
7 _____
8 _____
9 _____
10 _____
11 _____
12 _____
13 _____
14 _____
15 _____

16 _____
17 _____
18 _____
19 _____
20 _____
21 _____
22 _____
23 _____
24 _____
25 _____
26 _____
27 _____
28 _____
29 _____
30 _____

DAY THREE: CELEBRATING YOU

When was the last time that you stopped and took a moment to celebrate and reward yourself?

_____

_____

_____

_____

What is your favorite way to be good to yourself?

_____

_____

_____

DAY FOUR: CELEBRATING YOU

"The more you **seize** the **opportunity** to celebrate your life, the more **growth** there will be to celebrate. Take a minute and **praise** yourself for **every** step towards a **better** you."

~ Reea Rodney

The more you celebrate yourself the more your confidence raises. List 5 major life accomplishments that you're proud to have achieved.

1. _____

2. _____

3. _____

4. _____

5. _____

How can you celebrate you in a way that's meaningful?

_____

_____

_____

_____

DAY FIVE: CELEBRATING YOU

The Most...

(Fill in the Blanks)

The most proud of me I've ever been was...

_____

_____

The most joyful I've ever been was...

_____

_____

The most praise I gave myself was because...

_____

_____

The most rewarding season of my life was...

_____

_____

The most honoring moment I can remember was...

_____

_____

The most rewarding festivities I loved were...

_____

_____

DAY SIX: CELEBRATING YOU

Write a letter:

Write a letter to your future self. Remind your future self just why it's important to celebrate you.

END OF THE WEEK JOURNAL

1. What did you learn about yourself this week?

_____

_____

2. What areas will you improve?

_____

_____

3. What goals have you set as a result of this week's lesson?

_____

_____

4. What steps will you take to achieve your goals?

_____

_____

5. Are you committed to achieving your goals, If yes why?

_____

_____

_____

WEEK ELEVEN FOCUS: GRATITUDE

I've been told that "Gratitude is the key to living a happy and fulfilled life." I cannot begin to express how true this sentiment is. Show yourself some gratitude as well as others. It's amazing how positive people will become when they feel appreciated. Think of how you feel when someone shows you a measure of gratitude. What impact did that have in your life?

This week take a moment to thank yourself and others. Then, reflect on the impact of your expression of gratitude. You'd be amazed how better, happier, and more fulfilled you'll feel.

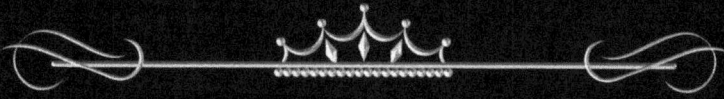

GRATITUDE

makes sense of our past, brings

PEACE

for today, and creates a vision for

TOMORROW

~ Melody Beattie

DAY ONE: GRATITUDE

1. What does gratitude looks like for you?

_____

_____

_____

_____

2. What is your favorite way you epxress thankfulness and gratitude to those around you?

_____

_____

_____

_____

DAY TWO: GRATITUDE

Thank You Note To Yourself
Write yourself a thank you note. Be sure to read it daily.

DAY THREE: GRATITUDE

Count your blessings.
List 30 things that you are grateful and thankful for.

1	16
2	17
3	18
4	19
5	20
6	21
7	22
8	23
9	24
10	25
11	26
12	27
13	28
14	29
15	30

DAY FOUR: GRATITUDE

"**Rejoice** ever more. **Pray** without ceasing. In every thing **give thanks**: for this is the will of God in **Christ Jesus** concerning you."

~ 1 Thessalonians 5:16-18

Pay It Forawrd
Pay it forward by writing a note of gratitude to your loved ones.

_____

_____

_____

_____

_____

_____

_____

_____

_____

_____

DAY FIVE: GRATITUDE

I AM GRATEFUL FOR...   (Fill in the blanks)

In my family, I am grateful for... _____

_____

_____

In my work place, I am grateful for... _____

_____

_____

In my neighborhood, I am grateful for... _____

_____

_____

Amongst my friends, I am grateful for... _____

_____

_____

In my church, I am grateful for... _____

_____

_____

DAY SIX: GRATITUDE

THANK YOU

is the best prayer that anyone could say. Thank you expresses extreme

GRATITUDE,
HUMILITY

and understanding."
~ Alice Walker

What do you think Alice Walker means by her inspirational quote above?

_____

_____

_____

_____

END OF THE WEEK JOURNAL

1. What did you learn about yourself this week?

_____

_____

_____

2. What areas will you improve?

_____

_____

_____

3. What goals have you set as a result of this week's lesson?

_____

_____

_____

4. What steps will you take to achieve your goals?

_____

_____

_____

5. Are you committed to achieving your goals, If yes why?

_____

_____

_____

_____

WEEK TWELVE FOCUS: FLOURISHING

Wow. What an incredible journey we've embarked on for the past 11 weeks. Hopefully, by now you've learned how to love, celebrate, and appreciate who you are. Again, the goal of this journal is to empower you, and that's what this week is all about.

This week, you will analyze several things designed to challenge you to continue to grow. Because we all are continually evolving, you will review your notes from the prior weeks (you're welcomed to revise some of your entries) and use them to create an action plan. Ultimately, we want you to be the BEST version of you.

We blossom under

PRAISE

like flowers in sun
and dew; we open,
we reach, we

GROW

~ Gerhard E Frost

DAY ONE: FLOURISHING

1. What elements made the circumstances where you blossom and grow?

_____

_____

_____

_____

2. What could you do to flourish where you are right now?

_____

_____

_____

_____

DAY TWO: FLOURISHING

1. Make a list of 30 things that make you happy. Things that help you blossom and bloom where you are.

1 _____

2 _____

3 _____

4 _____

5 _____

6 _____

7 _____

8 _____

9 _____

10 _____

11 _____

12 _____

13 _____

14 _____

15 _____

16 _____

17 _____

18 _____

19 _____

20 _____

21 _____

22 _____

23 _____

24 _____

25 _____

26 _____

27 _____

28 _____

29 _____

30 _____

DAY THREE: FLOURISHING

What voices are you hearing or lies you are believing that are like weeds, choking you where you stand?

_____

_____

_____

_____

What truths do you need to believe about yourself so you can begin to bloom again?

_____

_____

_____

_____

DAY FOUR: FLOURISHING

"You're under no **obligation** to be who people think you are. Change, **grow**, **rearrange** yourself. **Free** and beautiful things always **bloom** and **spark** with no holding back."

~ Charlotte Eriksson

What do you think of the quote above by Charlotte Erisson? How do you think this applies to your life?

DAY FIVE: FLOURISH

My Blooming Moments...
(Fill in the Flowers with moments where you blossomed)

DAY SIX: FLOURISH

"Just like

WILDFLOWERS

you must allow yourself to grow in all the places people thought you never would."

what are some places you grew and blossomed well where others thought you wouldn't?

_____

_____

_____

_____

what did it take to grow and blossom in those places?

_____

_____

_____

_____

_____

END OF THE WEEK JOURNAL

Now that you've completed the 12 weeks journal, where do you go from here? Excellent question! It's time to create an action plan. Take a moment and review the goals and steps to achieve the goals that you've written over the past 12 weeks. Now answer the following questions and don't forget to download your Free Goal Setting Worksheet Kit: www.coachreea.com/goal-setting-activity

Now answer the following questions:

1. What goals have you set for yourself?

_____

_____

_____

2. What steps will you take to achieve your goals?

_____

_____

_____

3. Do you have an accountability partner with whom you can share your goals with? If not, please find one or two.

_____

_____

_____

4. How often would you like your accountability partner to follow up with you on your progress? (I suggest once a week)

_____

_____

_____

END OF THE WEEK JOURNAL

Continued....

5. Write an affirmation statement that will motivate you to stay on this journey of self-empowerment.

"Love is **patient**, love is **kind**. It does not envy, it does not boast, it is not proud. It does not dishonor others, it is not self-seeking, it is not easily angered, it keeps no record of wrongs. Love does not delight in evil but **rejoices** with the **truth**. It always **protects**, always **trusts**, always **hopes**, always **perseveres**."

~ 1 Corinthians 13:4-7

Meet the Author
COACH REEA RODNEY

Reea Rodney is a wife and mother of three wonderful children who resides in Brooklyn, New York. Originally from Trinidad & Tobago, a small twin island located in the West Indies, she migrated to the United States in 2006 in pursuit of a better life for her family. In addition, Reea is also an Empowerment Life Coach, Children's Author, Motivational Speaker, a Childcare Provider and a Medical Assistant.

Because of her innate passion and desire to help children, Reea was inspired to write children's books via her publishing company, Dara Publishing LLC. She wanted to assist not only the children who were under her care, but children all over the world. Fueled by this purpose, Reea became a Certified Life Coach. The result? Dara Wisdom and Empowerment Coaching. In addition, Reea aspires to be a positive voice of empowerment for children that she herself lacked when she was a child.

She seeks to educate parents and young children through her dynamic mini workshops and self-improvement workbooks. Topics such as Self-Esteem, Self-Love, Self-Celebration, Self-Confidence and Bullying are topics that Reea addresses through her programs. While most of these life skills are not taught in schools they are valuable to a child's overall wellbeing and development.

"Put on your full amour and walk in your **PURPOSE** You were created for greatness and you are destined to win. Tap into your power source and **SHINE**

~ Reea Rodney

Email: coachreea@gmail.com
Websites: www.coachreea.com
Phone: 1-347-962-8363
Facebook: @reearodney1
Instragram: @darawisdomandempowerment

www.ingramcontent.com/pod-product-compliance
Lightning Source LLC
Chambersburg PA
CBHW062045090426
42740CB00016B/3025